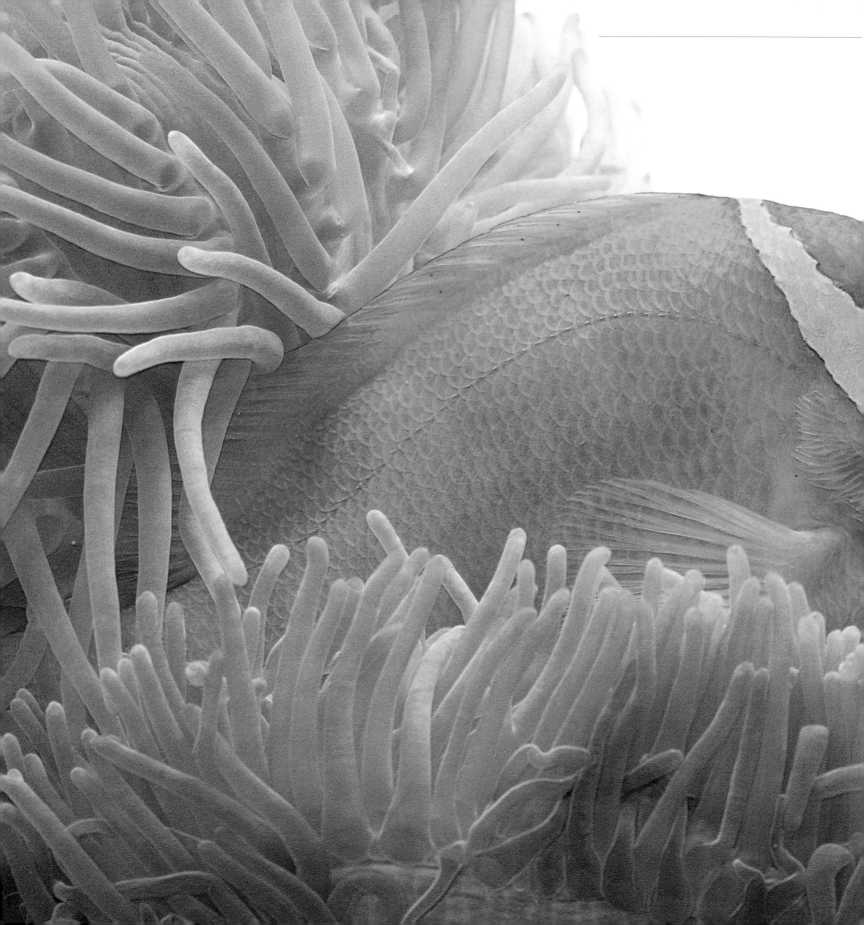

LOOK CLOSER

CORAL REEF

PHOTOGRAPHED BY
JANE BURTON

WRITTEN BY
BARBARA TAYLOR

DORLING KINDERSLEY . LONDON . NEW YORK . STUTTGART

DK

A DORLING KINDERSLEY BOOK

Project editor Christiane Gunzi **Project art editor** Val Wright Heneghan

Editorial assistant Deborah Murrell **Designer** Julie Staniland
Design assistant Nicola Rawson

Production Louise Barratt
Illustrations Nick Hall, Nick Hewetson, Dan Wright
Additional editorial assistance Jill Somerscales

Managing editor Sophie Mitchell
Managing art editor Miranda Kennedy

Consultants
Paul Clarke, Mandy Holloway
Charles Hussey, Bryan Pilkin, Kathie Way

With thanks to Neil Welton of Dorking Aquatic Centre,
who supplied the animals photographed in this book

First published in Great Britain in 1992 by
Dorling Kindersley Limited
9 Henrietta Street
Covent Garden
London WC2E 8PS

A CIP catalogue for this book is available from the British Library.
ISBN 0 86318 774 9

Colour reproduction by Colourscan, Singapore
Printed and bound in Italy by New Interlitho, Milan

CONTENTS

Look for us; and we will show you the size of every animal and plant that you read about in this book.

LIFE ON A CORAL REEF

CORAL REEFS TEEM WITH a rich variety of wildlife, from speedy shrimps and frilly sea slugs, to giant clams and schools of brightly coloured fish. A coral reef takes thousands of years to form. It is built up from the skeletons of tiny animals called corals. Corals can only survive in clean, warm, salty water which is shallow enough to allow sunlight to reach them. Coral reefs all over the world are threatened, mainly because of pollution and overfishing. We must protect all these coral reef animals if they are to survive.

Sea horse
Hippocampus kuda
12 cm long

Giant blue clam
Tridacna maxima
15 cm long

Clown fish
Amphiprion species
4 cm long

Sea slug
Elysia crispata
2.5 cm long

Sea anemone
Heteractis malu
10 cm wide

Hermit crab
Dardanus megistos
body and shell
8 cm long

Clown fish
Amphiprion species
17 cm long

Common octopus
Octopus vulgaris
24 cm long, including
tentacles

**Emperor angelfish
(young)**
*Pomacanthus
imperator*
6 cm long

Mandarin fish
Synchiropus splendidus
8 cm long

**Emperor angelfish
(adult)**
*Pomacanthus
imperator*
12 cm long

Grape coral
Plerogyra sinuosa
tentacle 6 cm long

**Strawberry
shrimp**
*Lysmata
debelius*
3 cm long

Sea cucumber
Paracucumaria
18 cm long

HORSE OF THE SEA

IT IS HARD TO BELIEVE that the sea horse is a fish. It has a head like a horse, a pouch like a kangaroo, and a tail like a monkey, for holding on to things. A sea horse can change colour to match its habitat and hide from enemies. This is useful because it cannot swim fast to escape danger. These shy, peaceful creatures spend most of the day amongst the coral waiting for food, such as shrimps, to pass within reach. During courtship, sea horses dance with their tails twined together. The female lays her eggs in a pouch on the front of the male's body. The eggs develop inside the pouch and the young emerge after two to seven weeks. As soon as they are born, young sea horses must fend for themselves.

DROPPING ANCHOR

The sea horse uses its strong, supple tail to anchor itself firmly to corals, seaweeds, and sponges on the reef. This helps to stop it being thrown about and injured by waves or underwater currents.

The fin on the back beats as many as 20 to 35 times a second.

These small fins look like ears. The sea horse flaps them to steer itself through the water.

To rise up, the sea horse straightens its tail. It curls its tail to sink.

The sea horse's eyes move independently, so it can look in two directions at once.

This see-through fin on the back bends to and fro to push the sea horse slowly through the water.

Close up, you can see ridges where the bony plates under the skin join to form the skeleton.

The snout is long and hollow like a drinking straw.

GUESS WHAT?

A young sea horse eats up to 3,500 shrimps in a day and grows more than twice its size in less than a month.

NOISY EATER

The sea horse has no teeth and swallows its food whole. It sucks up shrimps with its long, hollow jaws, making a clicking noise which can be heard some distance away. Sea horses feed most of the time during the day. They eat enormous amounts but have no stomach to store food in.

REEF BUILDERS

THESE BEAUTIFUL GRAPE corals may look like unusual plants, but they are really carnivorous (meat-eating) animals. Corals are related to jellyfish and sea anemones. Like them, they use stinging cells to defend themselves and catch their food. A coral colony like this one is made up of hundreds of individual creatures, called polyps. The polyps divide into two over and over again to form exact copies of themselves. They also produce eggs which, when fertilized, develop into larvae. The larvae swim around in the sea until they reach a suitable spot to settle down and develop into adults. Over thousands of years, the skeletons of dead corals build up on top of each other to form a reef.

When this coral polyp is open, you can see its many smooth tentacles.

DEADLY HARPOONS
Corals cannot move, so they rely on the movement of the water to bring their food to them. The poisonous tentacles paralyze the prey, then pass it to the mouth. Each tentacle of this grape coral is about the size of your finger. It feeds at night, on microscopic animals.

Each polyp can close up and pull its tentacles back inside its body for protection.

BIG BLUE CLAM

THIS COLOURFUL giant clam is a soft-bodied animal called a mollusc, which lives inside a strong, hard shell. The shell is made of two halves which can open and close. A clam opens its shell when it is feeding and shuts it tight when danger threatens. Growing on the clam's body are millions of tiny green plants called algae. These plants absorb some of the clam's waste products and, in return, the clam feeds on some of the algae. It also eats microscopic plants and animals called plankton which drift past in the sea water. Clams develop from tiny eggs which hatch into larvae. The larvae swim around for about nine days, then begin to grow into adults. Giant clams do not move once they are adult, and they sometimes grow as large as one metre across.

SUPER SIPHON
Clams have no head so they cannot breathe and feed in the same way as humans do. Instead they have two openings called siphons. A small siphon allows water full of oxygen and food to pass into the body, and a larger siphon squirts waste materials out of the body.

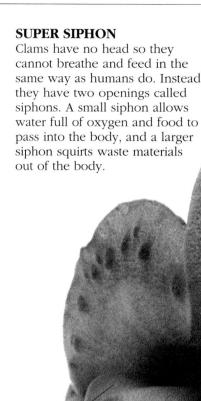

Waste products leave the body through this siphon.

The two sides of the mantle can join together so that the clam's body is completely enclosed and cannot be seen by predators.

Ridges and grooves on the shell make it strong. They also help to disguise the clam when it closes its shell.

LIVING LARDER
The green patches on the clam are colonies (groups) of algae. Algae live in the part called the mantle, which is the frilly layer between the clam's soft body and the hard shell. The algae continue to grow and multiply throughout the clam's life, so it always has a good source of food.

GUESS WHAT?
Blue clams like this one can live for 100 years. During their lives they sometimes make pearls as big as golf balls. This takes 10 years or more.

HINGED HOME
The clam first makes its shell from chemicals in the water, then the mantle gradually adds layers of chalk to the shell to make it bigger. The shell supports and protects the clam's soft body. The matching halves are joined together with a hinge, and strong muscles close them together for protection. The body of the clam is also joined to the shell by muscles.

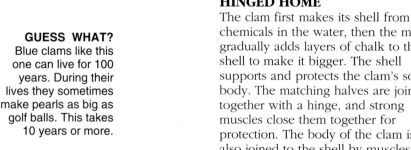
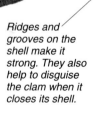

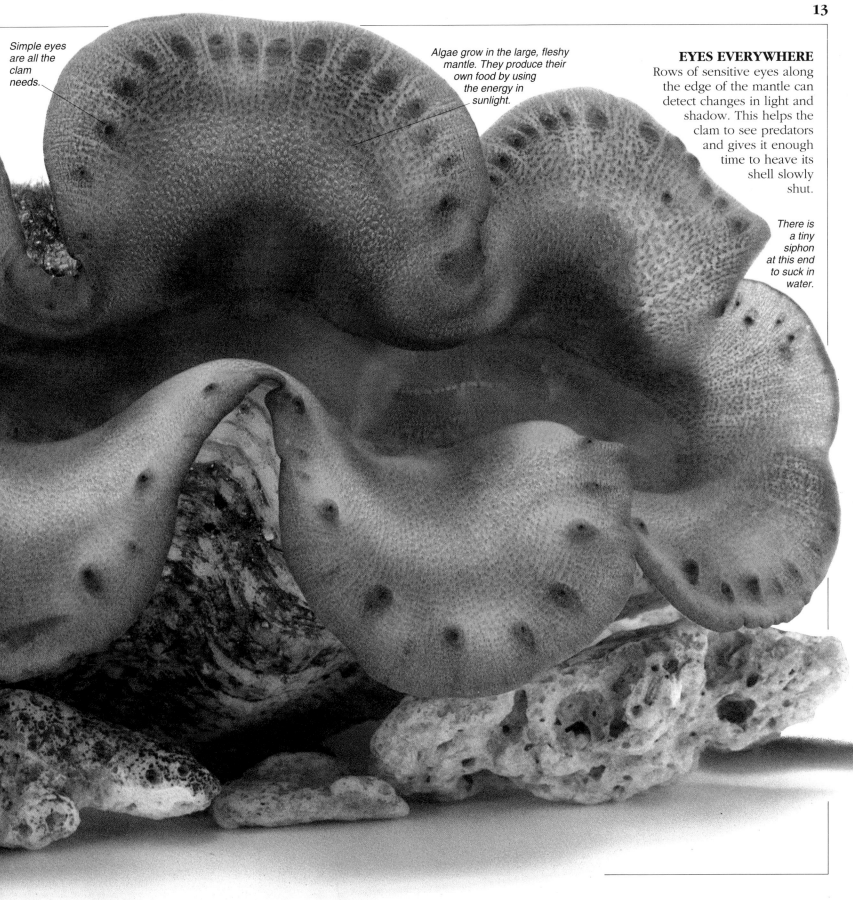

Simple eyes are all the clam needs.

Algae grow in the large, fleshy mantle. They produce their own food by using the energy in sunlight.

EYES EVERYWHERE
Rows of sensitive eyes along the edge of the mantle can detect changes in light and shadow. This helps the clam to see predators and gives it enough time to heave its shell slowly shut.

There is a tiny siphon at this end to suck in water.

SECOND-HAND HOME

THIS EXTRAORDINARY CRAB spends its life inside another animal's home. Hermit crabs like this one protect the soft rear part of their body, called the abdomen, by living in the empty shells of whelks and other sea snails. The coiled abdomen fits inside the shell, and a hook on the end helps the crab to keep a firm grip on it. The crab can stretch its legs out of the shell to pull itself along. It takes its home with it wherever it goes. When the crab grows too big for one shell, it simply moves to a larger one. Female hermit crabs lay eggs, which they carry around on one side of the abdomen. The eggs hatch into tiny larvae, which drift in the sea with the plankton. Finally, the larvae develop into adults and find a second-hand home of their own.

Bright dots on the body help to disguise the crab on the coral reef.

Special hairs called setae help the crab to feel its way around. They also detect the movements of predators or food in the water.

If danger threatens, the crab can quickly pull its whole body back inside this conch shell for protection.

NEW CLOTHES FOR OLD
The hard outer skin called the exoskeleton is on the front part of the body. It does not expand as the crab grows. Instead, the crab moults (sheds) its exoskeleton from time to time. A soft new exoskeleton grows beneath the old one, which splits so that the crab can pull itself out. The new exoskeleton soon hardens.

GUESS WHAT?
There are many different kinds of hermit crabs. Some are only the size of a pea, and others are as big as your hand.

HOUSE HUNTING
Hermit crabs have to search for an empty shell which is the right size. Before moving house, they investigate and explore the shell with their claws to see if it is large enough. Some hermit crabs live inside tubes in coral or wood instead of shells.

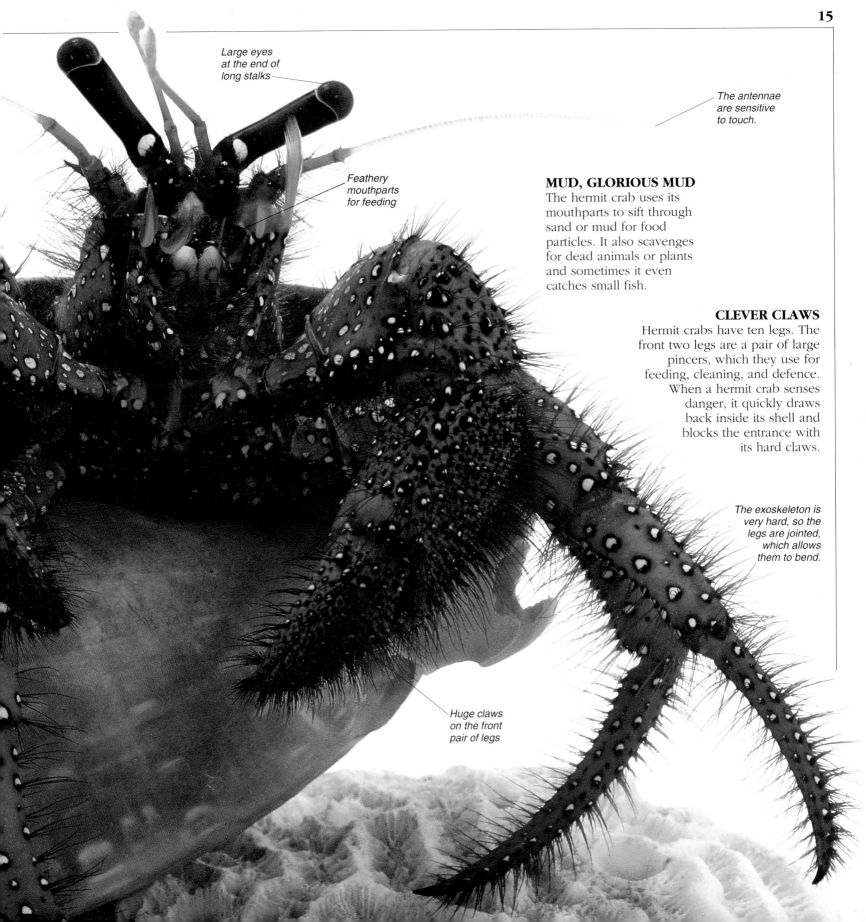

Large eyes
at the end of
long stalks

The antennae
are sensitive
to touch.

Feathery
mouthparts
for feeding

MUD, GLORIOUS MUD
The hermit crab uses its
mouthparts to sift through
sand or mud for food
particles. It also scavenges
for dead animals or plants
and sometimes it even
catches small fish.

CLEVER CLAWS
Hermit crabs have ten legs. The
front two legs are a pair of large
pincers, which they use for
feeding, cleaning, and defence.
When a hermit crab senses
danger, it quickly draws
back inside its shell and
blocks the entrance with
its hard claws.

The exoskeleton is
very hard, so the
legs are jointed,
which allows
them to bend.

Huge claws
on the front
pair of legs

CORAL REEF FRIENDS

CLOWN FISH LIVE IN HARMONY with other creatures called sea anemones. The sea anemone is related to jellyfish, and has poisonous tentacles for paralyzing prey. At the first sign of danger, a clown fish darts into the anemone's tentacles for safety. To protect itself from the poison, the clown fish covers itself with a layer of slimy mucus. The anemone also produces mucus to protect itself from its own sting. The clown fish lays its eggs and rears its young among the anemone's tentacles. Some kinds of sea anemones lay eggs, too. Others make smaller versions of themselves by dividing off part of their bodies.

GUESS WHAT?
Clown fish have never been seen living without sea anemones, but sea anemones can survive without clown fish.

TERRIBLE TENTACLES
The sea anemone grabs small creatures floating past in the water with its stinging tentacles. It also catches young fish and shrimps. The tentacles pass the prey down to the mouth opening, then spread out again to catch more food.

CLOWN COSTUME
The clown fish's bright colours mean that it cannot easily hide from enemies. But it can escape by swimming among the tentacles of the anemone, which makes it hard to catch. The colours and patterns of the fish may also warn predators of the anemone's poisonous tentacles, and help to keep both animals safe.

Each sea anemone has hundreds of stinging tentacles for catching food.

The fish's large eyes keep a look-out for danger.

A hard mouth for nibbling at algae on the coral reef

The base of the anemone's body is attached to a rock for support.

The side fins are used for steering and changing direction.

SHY STRAWBERRY

THIS STRAWBERRY SHRIMP is one of many kinds of tiny, brightly coloured shrimps which live on the coral reef. Strawberry shrimps are very shy and hide in natural crevices in the coral or dig burrows in the sand. A strong exoskeleton helps to protect their soft bodies. Shrimps have paddle-like back legs called swimmerets, which help them to swim fast. Female strawberry shrimps carry their eggs on these swimmerets. A sticky cement holds the eggs in place while they develop. After a few weeks the eggs hatch into larvae, and swim away from their mother. Eventually, the larvae change into tiny versions of their parents.

The shrimp uses these legs to preen its antennae.

BALANCING ACT

At the base of the antennae is a special organ called a statocyst, which helps the shrimp to balance. This organ is like a sac containing sand or grit. Each time the shrimp moves, the grit moves inside the sac. Cells in the sac send information to the brain, so it can work out which way up the shrimp is in the water.

There is a special organ for balancing inside here.

Each antenna is made up of lots of segments, so it can bend.

CLEANING SERVICE

The shrimp strains particles of food from the water with its fringed mouthparts. Strawberry shrimps are known as cleaners, because they use their mouthparts to remove parasites from the skin of fish. They also scavenge for dead animal or plant remains and catch living prey, such as plankton.

The two pairs of antennae detect chemicals in the water and help the shrimp to find food.

If the shrimp loses one of its claws, a new one grows to replace it.

The shrimp uses its claws called chelipeds to pick up food and dig in the sand.

GUESS WHAT?

During the day, cleaner shrimps like this one often group together in one place, to form special cleaning stations. Fish visit them so that the shrimps can clean them of parasites.

This jagged point on the carapace is called a rostrum. It juts out to protect the front of the head.

The two large compound eyes detect movements in the water.

The top part of the exoskeleton (the carapace) protects the front of the body called the thorax.

The shrimp's bright colours help fish recognize that this is a cleaner shrimp.

NEW SKIN FOR OLD

Strawberry shrimps grow rapidly in short bursts because they can only increase in size when they moult. They usually eat the old exoskeleton each time they moult because it contains nutritious salts. The soft new exoskeleton takes time to stretch and harden, so strawberry shrimps hide away from enemies, such as fish and crabs, until their new armour is strong.

Close-up, you can see lots of tiny hair-like setae covering the body.

A flexible, segmented abdomen allows the shrimp to swim backwards very rapidly.

Strawberry shrimps can walk slowly over the coral reef on their four pairs of long front legs.

CORAL REEF KALEIDOSCOPE

THE BRILLIANTLY COLOURED mandarin fish lives near the bottom of the sea. It spends most of its time hidden in crevices or cracks in the coral reef. The mandarin fish feeds on smaller fish and other creatures that swim or float past it in the water. It also nibbles at the algae on the coral reef with its hard mouth. The bold patterns on its skin help to protect the fish from enemies, by warning them of the bad-tasting slime called mucus that its body produces. The mandarin fish can also deter larger fish from attacking it by raising the long spine on its back. This trick makes the fish appear larger than it really is.

There are no eyelids or tear ducts on the eyes. The sea water cleans the eyes instead.

The small, downturned mouth is a good shape for nibbling food from the coral reef.

Bony covers protect the gills, which take in oxygen from the water.

This long, pointed spine is the first ray of the front fin on the fish's back. These back fins are called dorsal fins.

The tail fin moves from side to side to push and steer the fish through the water.

Both eyes stick out so that the fish can see in front and to the sides. Mandarin fish can see things in colour.

This ventral fin, together with the dorsal fin, helps the fish to stay upright in the water.

SIXTH SENSE
Like all fish, the mandarin fish has a line of pores, or holes, called the lateral line, along each side of the body. The lateral line contains special sense organs which detect movements and pressure changes in the water. These help the fish to find its way around and to sense danger or a possible meal.

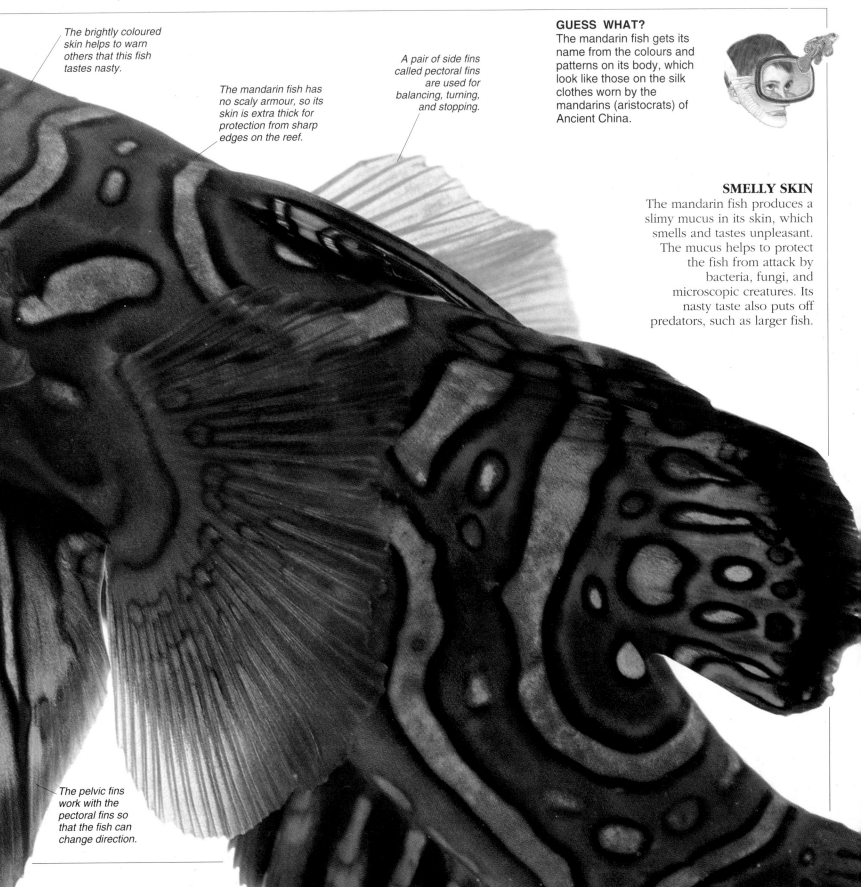

The brightly coloured skin helps to warn others that this fish tastes nasty.

The mandarin fish has no scaly armour, so its skin is extra thick for protection from sharp edges on the reef.

A pair of side fins called pectoral fins are used for balancing, turning, and stopping.

The pelvic fins work with the pectoral fins so that the fish can change direction.

GUESS WHAT?
The mandarin fish gets its name from the colours and patterns on its body, which look like those on the silk clothes worn by the mandarins (aristocrats) of Ancient China.

SMELLY SKIN
The mandarin fish produces a slimy mucus in its skin, which smells and tastes unpleasant. The mucus helps to protect the fish from attack by bacteria, fungi, and microscopic creatures. Its nasty taste also puts off predators, such as larger fish.

CRAWLING CUCUMBER

SAUSAGE-SHAPED SEA CUCUMBERS crawl over the coral
reef on their tube feet picking up particles of food with their
sticky tentacles. These remarkable animals are related to starfish
and sea urchins, and they have lived on Earth for millions of
years. A sea cucumber can change its colour and its size. It has
no head, just a mouth at one end and an opening called an anus
at the other end. Sea cucumbers have bendy bodies with leathery
skin and some can produce poisonous, sticky threads to trap
enemies. They lay eggs which develop into larvae. The larvae are
small and transparent and drift along in the sea. Sea cucumbers
lay thousands of eggs because many of the larvae will be
eaten and only a few survive to develop into adults.

GUESS WHAT?
To save their skin, some
sea cucumbers can split
their body wall and push
out their internal organs.
Their skin is all that is
left. The sea cucumber
grows a new set of
insides in a few weeks.

*This opening, called the
anus, gets rid of waste
materials. The sea
cucumber also uses it
for breathing.*

FEATHERY FEELERS
Around the mouth there are many
large, feathery tentacles. They are
covered with a sticky substance
called mucus. The tentacles feel for
tiny plants and animals on the
coral reef and the sea cucumber
sucks the food off the tentacles
with its fleshy lips.

*The feathery shape
of the tentacles
helps them to
catch as much
food as possible.*

*Particles of food
catch on the sticky
mucus which covers
each tentacle.*

Sea cucumbers can pull these tentacles back inside the body for protection.

The mouth is in the middle of the tentacles.

The tough skin has spines to persuade enemies not to eat the sea cucumber.

Suckers on the ends of the tube feet grip on to rocks as the sea cucumber walks.

WALKING ON THE WATER

Many sea cucumbers have rows of brightly coloured tube feet along the sides of their bodies. Water fills the tube feet so that they become stiff and work like levers to push the sea cucumber along over the rocks. Suckers on the ends of the feet grip on to rocks and other slippery surfaces.

Each tube foot is full of water.

TOP OF THE CLASS

OCTOPUSES ARE CLEVER animals that can learn and remember things. They are shy, and spend most of their time shuffling around on the coral reef or hiding inside their home, which they build from a pile of stones. This common octopus sometimes lurks inside coral caves and jumps out on crabs and shellfish as they pass by. Octopuses are related to molluscs such as clams, but they do not have a shell and they can swim much faster than most shellfish. A female octopus lays long strings of eggs and hangs them from the roof of her home. She keeps the eggs clean and guards them so carefully that she does not have time to feed herself. After about six weeks the eggs hatch into tiny octopuses and soon afterwards the female octopus dies of starvation.

ARMS EVERYWHERE

An octopus has eight writhing arms with strong suckers which curl around its victims to stop them from escaping. The octopus bites its prey with a horny beak, and injects it with poisons and special juices to make it easier to digest. Then the octopus uses its file-like tongue, called a radula, to tear off pieces of flesh.

GUESS WHAT?
When it is disturbed, an octopus shoots a cloud of black ink called sepia into the water. This confuses a predator so that the octopus has time to escape.

Scientists believe this blue spot helps the octopus to recognize another of its kind.

The arms feel and taste things. They are also used for walking and holding food.

Strong suckers down each arm help the octopus to hold on to rocks and food.

The funnel helps to propel the octopus along in the water.

THE JET SET

The octopus swims by jet propulsion. It squeezes a jet of water out of the funnel and this pushes it through the water. The hot gases rushing out of the back of a jet engine push an aeroplane forwards in a similar way. The octopus can steer itself in the water by directing the jet stream.

Each sucker has millions of microscopic hairs for feeling surfaces.

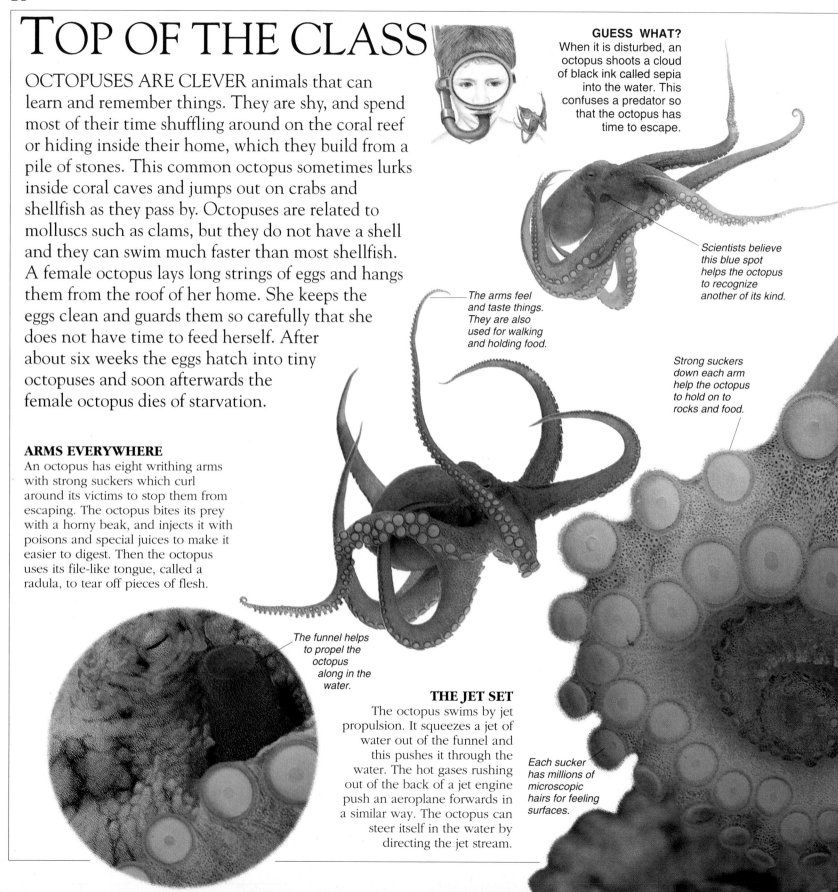

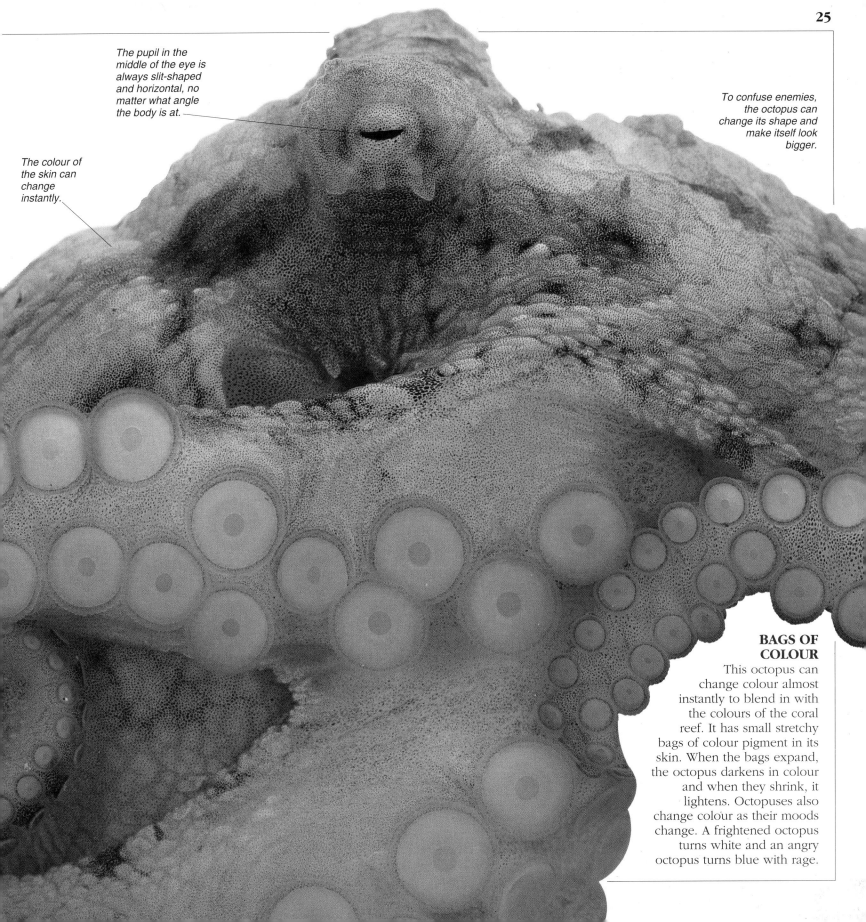

The pupil in the middle of the eye is always slit-shaped and horizontal, no matter what angle the body is at.

To confuse enemies, the octopus can change its shape and make itself look bigger.

The colour of the skin can change instantly.

BAGS OF COLOUR

This octopus can change colour almost instantly to blend in with the colours of the coral reef. It has small stretchy bags of colour pigment in its skin. When the bags expand, the octopus darkens in colour and when they shrink, it lightens. Octopuses also change colour as their moods change. A frightened octopus turns white and an angry octopus turns blue with rage.

STRIPED ANGELS

THE EMPEROR ANGELFISH hovers in the water near small caves in the coral reef. This is so that it can dart inside if it senses danger. Its thin body allows it to slip easily through narrow gaps in the coral. This agile fish spends most of the day nibbling at sponges on the reef. Once two angelfish have mated, they remain together for the rest of their lives. The pair live in their own territory, a small patch of the reef which they defend against other angelfish. The female lays eggs which are fertilized by the male. The eggs float in the sea, away from the reef and the many enemies which might eat them. Larvae hatch out of the eggs, and eventually change into little fish.

COLOURFUL SIGNALS

The vibrant colours and patterns of this adult emperor angelfish help it to recognize others of its own kind. Colours can also attract a mate, and may become brighter in the breeding season. Angelfish usually live in water at least 15 metres deep where their bright colours show up well in the dim light.

There is one eye on each side of the head for good all-round vision.

This spine below the gill cover can lock the fish into a crevice so that an enemy cannot pull it out backwards.

The strong teeth inside the mouth pull pieces of sponge, coral, and microscopic plants called algae, from the reef.

These pectoral fins are for balancing and turning.

The tail fin is called the caudal fin. It pushes the fish along and helps with steering.

SCHOOL UNIFORM

Young emperor angelfish have blue bodies with white circles. They often swim in groups, called schools, and their uniform appearance helps to protect them from attack by the adults. The colours of the young fish are very different from those of the adults, and they change gradually as they grow older.

GUESS WHAT?
Large adults can make a loud thumping sound which may startle a diver. Scientists are not sure how they produce this sound.

These light-coloured rings attract predators to the tail end rather than the head end, so that if they attack, they do not harm the head.

Close-up, you can see the overlapping scales which protect the body.

The dark blue colour and light pattern help to disguise the young fish from enemies.

A narrow snout for reaching into crevices in the coral

LETTUCE SLUG

SEA SLUGS ARE RELATED to garden snails, but they have no shell to protect their soft bodies. Most kinds of sea slug have very special diets. Some eat only a few types of sponge, while others feed on coral or even other sea slugs. This lettuce slug feeds on tiny green plants called algae. Like snails, sea slugs scrape up food with their strong jaws and a special tongue called a radula which works like a nail file. Sometimes they mix up the food with slimy mucus and suck it up instead. Each sea slug is both male and female at the same time. This makes it easier for them to find a mate and it means that every sea slug can lay eggs. The eggs hatch into larvae which swim around until they find a good place to grow into adults.

GUESS WHAT?
Some kinds of sea slugs steal poisonous stinging cells from the sea anemones that they feed on, and use them for their own defence.

This frilly edge to the body is for breathing and catching sunlight.

The bright green colour shows that this slug eats plants called algae.

The soft body has no shell for protection.

A sea slug crawls over the slippery seaweed on its flat, slimy foot.

TERRIBLE TASTE
Lettuce slugs may look like a tasty salad, but they have special glands in their skin which produce a bad-tasting substance so that predators do not try to eat them.

LETTUCE LEAF

In order to breathe, the lettuce slug takes in air through its skin. The algae in its skin capture sunlight and turn it into energy by a process called photosynthesis. So the sea slug's skin is rather like the leaf of a plant.

There is an eye at the base of each tentacle.

Special fat tentacles for smelling food

GLOSSARY

Abdomen *the rear part of the body*
Algae *simple plants such as seaweed*
Antennae *a pair of feelers*
Carapace *the top part of the exoskeleton*
Carnivorous *meat-eating*
Exoskeleton *an outer covering on the body, made of a substance called chitin*
Larvae *grubs, which will later develop into adults*
Mandibles *jaws*
Microscopic *too small to see without a microscope*
Molluscs *soft-bodied animals which often have shells, such as slugs and snails*
Moult *to shed the skin or exoskeleton*
Mucus *a slimy, often poisonous substance which certain animals produce*

Parasite *a plant or animal which lives in or on another living thing*
Photosynthesis *the use of sunlight by plants to produce the energy to grow*
Plankton *microscopic sea creatures and plants*
Polyps *the tiny individual animals whose skeletons make up the coral reef*
Predator *a meat-eating hunter*
Prehensile tail *a tail which can grasp hold of plants and rocks*
Radula *a file-like tongue*
Setae *special hairs on the body*
Tentacles *flexible feelers for touching, feeding, or smelling*
Thorax *the front part of the body, containing the heart and lungs*